TANKA &ME

Other titles by Kaethe Schwehn

Tailings: A Memoir

The Mineral Point Poetry Series

Tanka & Me   Kaethe Schwehn
My Seaborgium   Alicia Rebecca Myers
Fair Day in an Ancient Town   Greg Allendorf
My Tall Handsome   Emily Corwin

MINERAL POINT POETRY SERIES   NO. 1

Kiki Petrosino, Editor

TANKA &ME poems
Kaethe Schwehn

Brain Mill Press · Green Bay, Wisconsin

Some of these poems have appeared previously in the following publications:

Clementine, Issue 3: "From Her Deathbed . . ."

Crazyhorse, Fall 2007: "Pammy and Tanka," "Me to Tanka [Tanka, It Is Me]."

"Tanka to Me [Try Gentle]" appeared in *A Sing Economy* (FlimForum Press, 2008).

Published in the United States by Brain Mill Press.

ISBN 978-1-942083-10-8

Cover photograph © Leann McDaniel.
Cover design by Stray King Design.
Interior illustration by Ann O'Connell.
Interior design by Williams Writing, Editing & Design.

www.brainmillpress.com

The Mineral Point Poetry Series, number 1.

Published by Brain Mill Press, the Mineral Point Series is edited by Kiki Petrosino. In odd years, the series invites submissions of poetry chapbooks around a theme. In even years, the editor chooses a full collection.

for Peder

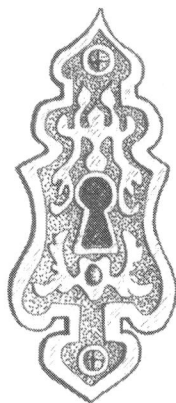

Contents

Foreword

You might be forgiven, on first opening this chapbook, for experiencing a bit of confusion at the seeming disparity between the collection's title and the form of the poems contained herein. A *tanka* is a kind of Japanese short lyric, rigidly structured. *Tanka* is also a category of Japanese sword, the name of a mountain in Peru, and a type of exquisite Tibetan Buddhist painting on silk.

But *Tanka & Me* doesn't traffic in any of these traditional tankas.

The amazement of this collection is found not in the poems' mere *refusal to be tankas* but in the fact that, by *refusing to be only one thing*, the poems seem to claim dominion over multiple categories of utterance. These are ravenous poems of love and identity, audacious in their movement across the landscape of the page. From the first piece, we're transported to a place that is neither wonderland nor underworld, but a site of astonishment elaborated by the speaker's hyper-keen vision:

> The lily pads graft hairs into the murk,
> Cotton candy petals drooping under thick grey sky.

To be sovereign over such territory requires a unique subjectivity, one capable of falling in love with cotton candy and murk. Tanka emerges as the speaker's witchy alter ego, a being of pure energy who "sways a trance" that draws speaker (and reader) through the "keyhole" of the "neck," which is to say: directly into the mind, where reckonings begin.

I'm afraid of Tanka. I also love her. In these poems, we watch her "tooling through pools of ions," "ripping chives out of their earthen sockets," and driving a Corvette whose trunk contains "an ice pick, an owl, a lozenge, and a turbine." Her riotous adventures contrast the staid domestic routines of the speaker, who identifies herself as "a Midwestern white girl living in a town / where a bank raid is reenacted every year." Throughout this series of poems, the almost-video-game theatrics of Tanka's otherworldly existence are juxtaposed with concrete changes in the speaker's earthly life; namely, her love for a decidedly human man and her mixed feelings about their impending marriage:

> Sometimes I want to lay my body on him
> and smother him up like a gauze sandwich.

> Sometimes I think he is the black knight in a certain
>   other story.
> That maybe he should just befriend the puma and
>   leave me be.

It is the relationship between Tanka and the speaker, these two lyric phantoms (who, after all, represent different aspects of what it means to be complexly female, to be both warmly and cruelly bodied in our world) that constitutes the central dynamism—the core of love—that these poems contemplate. These poems celebrate the wild inner self, the glittering products of an imaginative life well lived. Some of the most moving moments in this series take place when the two figures converse in dialogue. In "Me and Tanka," Tanka asks:

> *Then how did you make me?*
> she says.
> *Grace,*
> I say.

Oh,
she says.
I don't feel much grace inside me.

Me neither,
I say.

Always, Tanka appears a creature of infinite potential. While the speaker sometimes loses herself in doubt, Tanka has her tools and knows how to use them. Her confidence is dangerous and enticing. The image of the owl, in particular, placed in the trunk of her Corvette like a component belonging to any roadside emergency kit, is perhaps an homage to the moment in Alice Notley's *Descent of Alette* in which Notley's speaker dons an owl mask in order to do battle with "the tyrant," her adversary. But in the world of *Tanka & Me,* the owl's totemic power is just one tool among many for quelling the too-loud voices—those outer and inner "tyrants"—that dare to tell us what women's lives *can't* or *shouldn't* be.

Let the roar of Tanka's turbines silence all doubt.

Kiki Petrosino
Editor, Mineral Point Poetry Series

TANKA
&ME

Tanka and You

Tanka snaps her fingers and there you are upon
a boat. Alone. Wooden. Paddleless. As you have been

for hours. The lily pads graft hairs into the murk,
cotton candy petals drooping under thick gray sky.

Not anything moving that's alive.
Not animals or insect dust.

The water makes a back-throat chucking noise
against the boards. Half an inch of copper water

filled with leaf scabs lulls the ribs. A brown life vest, black
clasps, white mesh pockets, lies crumpled at the hull.

Your back returns to aching. The drizzling will not start.
Somewhere else, a school play's just beginning. Your
    daughter,

dressed as turnip, fiddles with a Band-Aid in the wings.
    What you would not give
for the unblurring of Mount Fuji at the camera lens's end:
    snow

chuffed from rock swirling upward into cloud-scudded
    sky,
blue swiveling through at cusp. Or Tanka barefoot

on a marble patio, filmy nightgown double-knotted at her
    hips.
She sways a trance. The thin cord loosens. Keyhole
    primed at neck.

The First Dusky Nun

Tanka grew ice pyramids inside her as a girl.

On June 12th, 2003, when she ribbed a dead possum
    with a stick
the pyramids shattered into glass pieces (frail,
    electron-sized)
and lodged inside her small intestine.

Late afternoon, December 12th, Tanka passed the glass
    (not willingly)
through stomach, colon, and the boards of Lutheran
    church bench where she sat
(a theology-meteorology major, waiting patient to record
    a winter storm).

She made a mess.
Watering the holy ground with all the glass and blood
unearthed her standing with the Good.

Tanka was the first dusky nun. First one to hitch up habit
and crawl over low stone wall, razing jaw along the moss,
wanting dust of another body along her comet-sensitive
    bust.

This week she's banished underwater, where no dust
    comes.
Or bodies. Banished to games of chance with sharks and
    the knee-paw
knee-paw of the lousy upstairs neighbors.

You can love someone for a long time without knowing how.

Tanka's Brother Dies (And Afterward)

A funeral is full of might and pleas.
First the guests process, nostalgia thick
upon their lids like puffy paint.
Then the guests sit rigid,
beguiling like they knew his smile
and his Madeline Island kayak shirt.

Tanka wears the doily apron
and shuffles plates and casseroles.
Beet juice splashes on her skirt,
bleeds through to knee.
When Tanka pulls up skirt to pee,
the new beet birthmark bests the grief
with puddled Russian shape.

With index knuckle Tanka
fondles it, christens it with nickname "Belarus."

W

Three days later Tanka will not wash the beet stain
off her leg. She covers it with silver foil, takes egg basket
from the hook, goes marketing. The foil puckers. Tanka
buys eel and cod and violet mums. In kitchen she gnaws
on radishes and waits for tea-water to quicken, bending
to sniff the white gas flame. At noon she re-tapes foil to
    her knee.
"Belarus, cold pond," she croons, "I am a dowager now."

(And Afterward)

Tooling through pools of ions, Tanka
is useless as a dove. Her ions have stone
bridges, mini whorls of world, spilled hydrogen
architecture. Tanka thanks the ions for their charge
by lying prostrate on her bedroom rug.

Tanka's room is right angles, no harbored
sense of flux. Tanka's stuffed cats encrypt
one wall with silent meows. When brother dies
after a while sister politely dis-deigns to remember.
Skims the zest off ion pools instead.

Pammy and Tanka

Tanka butts through the doors of an Old West saloon
for steak and ale.
Pammy the waitress spoils her with onion
flowers, with vanilla Coke, with the daffodil
sprig in her buttonhole.

Tanka and Pammy spend the afternoon reenacting
every Western movie ever made:

First Tanka takes Pammy out to a farmstead. Pammy loops
her arm around a fence post and sobs while Tanka drives off.

Then Pammy hangs long johns on the line and Tanka
sneaks up behind her with a rifle.

Then Tanka overturns wooden tables in the house while
Pammy makes fritters in a jiffy. "Where in God's name
is the SYRUP?" Tanka shouts, and Pammy closes

her lips and thighs around Tanka to show how fast
sap comes if noon touches maple's softer parts.

Then Tanka forks hay and Pammy pets the lambs.

Then a gold prospector comes.

Then a war parts them and Pammy hides Tanka's
blood-stained letters inside her hollowed Bible.

Then, on a gun-flint-colored Sunday, come
the men looking for Pammy. The chickens
struggle in their roosting. Pammy screams.

Bellied in a trench, Tanka hears the news of Pammy's
death. Her tears clean her big man hands. She sprinkles
salt on the life line of her palm and licks it off.

Then Tanka back at the farmstead alone, ripping chives
out of their earthen sockets. The rubbery green stems
flex in the wind that carries Pammy's voice

back to us, quite softly. She sings a lullaby or a song about
whiskey or she repeats a certain name and if her voice gets

lost in the leaves and makes Tanka's hurting worse . . . well.
Well, that's what she came for, wasn't it?

Tanka as the Weight-Loss Champion

Look at me! I am lithe! I slide out
like a deer on ice skates, my small
wet nose slightly lifted! I am spindly.

You look at me and you think: quill.
You think: skinny-skein of dove gore.
I could snowboard now.
I could be a freckled girl looking past
her sintered board at the Pisan sun.
Kidding. I'm so thin I've lost my arms.

The host says: "Tanka, step on the scale,"
and there's me, toeing the metal as
though I grew up hollow. Which I did not.
I was Kraft-fed and sped my circles in
a cul-de-sac. Now I am a spankable thread,
a string of breath so thin you could
Chopin me between the keys of a piano.

On live TV I say: "I waved good-bye
to all the goopy-food, won a personal
gym and fluorescent water toys and
sweated it out with Raquel down at
the Ranch. The mountains were the
toughest part, how I had to pull down
the moon while all East Asia waited."

I used to pick up a glass tumbler in my paw
when I was a big girl and I'd break it.
Lucia would fork the pieces out and read me
The Merchant of Venice, how the quality
of mercy is not strained, et cetera.
Now I bed on spider webs,
mambo at the tip of whip crack.
Skinny-minny me says: "Less is more!"
I'm the feather-line traced along the thorax
of the foaming foal. I'm hay straw, but I've
got sweet tits so men come round to chew.
I rub my belly down.

Me and Tanka

I am a Midwestern white girl living in a town
where a bank raid is reenacted every year.

I sport yum-yum tassels on my nipples.
Blame is a flower. I know where it grows.

At work, the copier cannot read an object larger
    than a notebook.
I practice pushing buttons.
I practice looking patient in front of the mirror.

I practice spaceships.

Concubine is a word I learned for the SATs.

My fiancé and I pray before dinner.
We distribute name tags at church.

Couple resurrection with a spinning class.
Then a lot of sex with Israelites.

What if, at the critical moment, I can't remember
    the Heimlich maneuver?
This question circles me while I sleep.

I make love to a flounder.
I'm all ears and a liver.

Our golden-eyed dog snores under the bed while
    we watch *Law & Order.*
My brother almost died.
My sister stole a handbag.

Yesterday I cried at the jeweler's
because the wedding band looked too big around
   my finger.

In the trunk of my Corvette I have
an ice pick, an owl, a lozenge, and a turbine.

I want my voice to stop breaking.
I want to write something true.

I was gentle
when I went
to the bulrushes.
I was gentle
when I pulled
you out.

Tanka and Briar

Briar is a dream man. All the luckless girls try to squirrel
him away with e-mails, trailing their pheromones
behind them like Prigs at a tea party.

Tanka likes her Briar where he is, slouched
in mealy boxers, single. He scoots remote
through hordes of Viking games without mentioning
her brother. Briar works in fossil fuels.
That means weeks upon an oil rig then days
upon a couch. While he flips stations, Tanka files
down his nails, pushes back his cuticles.
They've ordered sausage on the pizza.

Later Briar takes her to a bar. They sit in lawn chairs
on a patch of Astroturf and listen to the train rails
tremble.

I don't do death, says Tanka.
Death does us, says Briar.
Don't want to be done, says Tanka.

Briar smells his hands,
pink and smooth with all her swaddling.
Briar takes her hands and folds
the Sunday sports section
over them.
Read this, he says.

Tanka in a State of Grace

pretty princess tiara
porridge forehead
tea spout nose
arachnid mole at edge of lip
poulticed molar
bowl cut chin
stark neck
(unrung with life preserver)
yellow slicker collarbone
limehair arms
bosom (what a crease to wonder!) bosom
desert
wand-smoothed belly
sequoia thighs
cherub knees
sea tendon calves
(squeezing the pollen from all)
in her water body
bird feet / boatless / no buoy

Me to Tanka

Tanka, it is
me walking the beach
among the dead bodies
of squid, their half-lemon
eyes inked black, getting in no sun.

The serpents twining below the sand
dune their bodies up. I climb one and sit beside
a patch of grass. Tanka, it occurs to me that this
is a heaven beach. The sheet of silver sky
and the sheet of silver water compliment
each other.
        "Nice ribs," says the sky.
        "Cute hairpins," says the sea.

The hairpins are thin white
bombs and the belly of the sea
explodes. Sand prickles the face of the sky.

The sea was being facetious, which I didn't think
was allowed in heaven.
Tanka, it is.

Tanka to Me

Try gentle.

Remember how tasty a
sandwich can be?

Sandblast your poems.
Start over.
This world's not any better
for Dover Beach.

There's a bitch trying
to write you a parking ticket.

Right where you thought
you'd be safe.

Think of the turtle
that appeared on your sun deck.

How the dog went mad
inside the house.

How she scratched her claws
against the windows.

How the turtle
didn't care. Ahhh . . . wet
wood said the turtle inside
her head.

Tanka as an Unaccompanied Minor

On this flight Tanka would like
seat 7A and a blowjob. Cockless,
she'll settle for a fine-fingered
man and a tray table soldiered
with alcohol. The view out her
porthole shows the luggage man's
radio, perched to the side of a belt
sliding into the DC-10's belly.

On this flight Tanka would like a bite
of Ms. Happy Stewardess PM
Stewardess PM shows Tanka where
the demonstration seat belts live.
Stewardess PM crawls down aisles
with a Taser in her mouth, gunning
the calves of all the sleeping mums.
Stewardess PM, why do you cackle
so happy when the cabin lights grow dim?

On this flight the Wise Men whisper in the row ahead.

On this flight a bucket-drum player, his sticks
the vertebrae of a giraffe, sounds out Masters
of War again, again.

On this flight everything happens in Tanka at once.
That is to say: her scalp folds back.
That is to say: God gets stuck inside her

and later her fingers cannot hook God out,
though she puts a water bottle on her belly, sighs,
grasps the sheet into her fists, fucks Briar,
fucks Briar again, befriends him, befriends
all the little animals, rills mascara down her
cheeks. Ding-dong! Still, it's God stuck and all this
obsidian breath filling every pustule of her, every
piranha she eclipses, every sushi move she makes.

And God likes dusk so much, God makes her
go out there. Out into that world.
Her nipples freeze. The beetles bite, one below
her navel. Go on out there, says God.
Tanka has diarrhea on every rhododendron on the block
until God mocks her into going home.

There, nestled, God soothes around her neck.
God swims through her thighs and calves and
hunkers down until her feet are mangers, until
they're swaddled tight. The huff of oxen warms
her toes. Then shrieking. Then a ticking bomb.
God loves.

Me to Tanka

Tanka, I'm here.
Over here where the fake knife is being
stuck into the fake loaf of raisin bread. Where
sunglasses dangle from a rhinestone cord.
If I were you, I would use that cord for evil.

Tanka, I'm here,
with thumbs and a sunflower napkin.
The Flick Creek fire is near but we remain
at evacuation level number two.
There is croquet and a well-watered lawn.
Bikes and a pocked-face road.

Tanka, over here it's the same old story.
I love a man but maybe not enough.

Sometimes I want to lay my body on him
and smother him up like a gauze sandwich.

Sometimes I think he is the black knight in a
    certain other story.
That maybe he should just befriend the puma and
    leave me be.

Sometimes we imagine our lives
together while we watch the clouds
form a big grey turtle. He says,
now the turtle will come and crush us
and this sort of comment makes it possible
for me to love him all the more.

Soon he will be buying me purple beads in Venice
and when I thrash my legs in ecstasy
they will not bump his, not even accidentally.

Tanka, sometimes I just want to know.
I want to scream wild
strawberries.

You chortle *tis the season!*
shoveling the deep white snow in front of you.

Tanka to Briar

I can be no clearer than this:

You are a mackerel sandwich and I am blessed infinity
stuffed into the roots of a violet.

You are a goose bump on the testicle of a hippopotamus.
You are a thin wet hair in an electrical socket.

You are thirteen minutes after the hour.
I am midnight.

You are a heel of raisin bread with mustard soaking into
    the crust.
I am the penultimate oyster.

You throw your head back in the barnyard. You wrap foil
around the wings of pigeons. You choose, again and
    again,
to behave as though you live in 17th-century Britain.

I choose the boxcar full of ferns.

You are salted percussion and
I am equestrian waterdance.

A pony has wings, I say
and you continue to grate the block of cheddar.

Look, you say
and my eyes rove past you, mirroring all the ghosts.

Let's make love, you say
and I am too drunk with stripes to answer.

What do you mean? you ask
and I take you to the field, to the glistening field.

You do not see it. You ask to understand it.
If you cannot see this, we are lost, I say.

If I cannot see this, I will have to follow closer, you reply.
You put your hand upon my hip.

The dragonflies sharpen their wings.

The Flood

Three days ago, when it began to rain, Tanka offered her open hands to him. She mimed filling a water jug. Then she mimed brushing a pony, pulling its foreleg back gently.

Now Tanka sits in a lawn chair on her roof watching the Ark disappear. Red banners attached to the mast ripple above the wake. Little white waves chuck the gray chin of the sea. The floodwaters have only risen to the upper sills.

On the Ark, there is the sound of harp music. Ham fashions a way to fry an egg. The sawdust coughs up as the bull shifts his weight. Noah's wife uses an oyster shell to carve a mark into the bow. The mark means: three days down. She drives a hole through the shell and wears it at her neck.

This far in all directions, Tanka can see the earth turning down. The moon tries to pull up the edges but the edges stay tucked under. Tanka walks down to her room and opens a window. She submerges her wrists in the water until she feels her neck grow cool. A spider web hangs in the nook of the window. Tanka lays her finger in as bait. As promised the brown spider comes and bites her.

Me and Tanka

Tanka, I say over lemonade, *I brought you to life.*
Please try to show some respect.

Tanka sticks out her tongue and then
holds it between her fingers.
I was born on a pirate ship, she repeats
again and again and again.

It is late afternoon.
The seashell mobile twirls above us on the porch.
Tanka has had three glasses of lemonade already.
I do not want her to have any more.
I do not know how to say *no.*

You have small tits, says Tanka,
let's play Twister.
No Tanka, I say, *I'm tired.*

You're dull, you mean, says Tanka.
I'm full of vixen tricks, she says.
Fine, I say.

I pull the stuffing out of cobras.
Good for you.

I paint cacti on teacups. I'm the muse
of brigadiers. I fashion a slug with a little
  mortarboard.
In his eye I sprig the gleam of triumph
or Rousseau.
I know, I say.

You're dull, she says, *you can't even
cross your eyes correctly. Your relationships last
five months because you turn so* USUAL.
*In your Secret Garden
you grow carrots and plastic wrap.
You like Lean Cuisine dinners.
You don't have fancy shoes.
You hum poorly. And you're dull.*
I know, I say.

Then how did you make me? she says.
Grace, I say.

Oh, she says. *I don't feel much grace inside me.*
Me neither, I say.

I start to cry a little.
I didn't see the sadness coming
and that makes me cry harder.

Tanka is quiet then.
We breathe.

At the Emerald Zoo

For me, it is like slogging
through vomit with a minnow net and
catching things up from the curdle:
a chunk of apple, a strand of lemon
grass, a beeswax candle
shaped like a whale. This, to me,
is marriage.

Tanka is trying to explain to Briar why,
when he got down on one knee beside
the snow rat cage just now, and offered
her his life, she had to bark out sharply
no and bite him on the earlobe, hard.

The snow rat's tail curves to the right
and then to the left. Briar is bereft. *I have waited*
so long, he says. *You asked me to join*
your cell phone plan.

A cloud rat has three eye teeth. Scientists believe
a cloud rat will fill his mouth with stones
if he is hungry or his mate is barren.

On the far side of the cage, an Emerald Zoo
employee pushes a rubber plunger
down to make sprayed rain. The snow rat
climbs to a fork in the tree and licks his paw.
He tucks his snout below his ribs. Pearly bits
of water bind to his fur and shine a
permanent nocturne.

Marie Curie knew.
Her fingers shook but something in
her bones awoke and so she leaned in closer.

No, no, no, no-no-no, says Tanka loudly.
Briar presses his forehead to the glass.
A breeze floats down the tunnel. On the
Tropical Trail, dolphins spit their sideways
tricks into the air. The cloud rat glows
like radium.

Plea

Tanka, help.
I am here museless.
Water in the glass
and no flower or pubis or mule in the glass to amuse me.
My students have white smiles and even the soft blond
hair at their brows is pulled back tightly.

I am becoming deathly afraid that I am normal.
That the neon hills that once erupted in my dreams
will not return.

Dina makes poems out of pigeons and periscopes.
She describes *what's framed in a transparent casket* so
	perfectly you want to baste it.

Zach has magic connective tissue in his brain.
He says two things like "birds in your eyes" and
	"fountain" and *zoom!* they waltz together tenderly.
Then there is Elizabeth who took "white" and "salt"
and said them over and over so beautifully that now the
	words belong in her camp.
They lay down and lick her goblets raw.

A blank sheet hangs between my temples. No surprises
	there.
I have a dog and a man and cable and a diamond ring.
I am content.

And the poet in me capsizes.
Tanka, which act is this?
Where are my scene notes?
Who will rescue me from the streamlined whiteness of
   this place where everyone is a stewardess and longing
   is an abstract term we discuss before making love?

The domestic is incontrovertible.

Happiness is glowing with her bitch sign.

From Her Deathbed, Tanka Addresses the World One Last Time

Old squeegee, old fit-to-kill, old
tar and feathered backgammon curl,
we had a good thing going for a while.

You put a muscle in the sun so he could ope his eye and
    glower at me.
I bronzed Baywatch and Malibu and wore
a white bikini with lime green spots.
I fished dead mice from the scaly grates of pools.
Dead, wet mice.
Slick little tubers.
I'd tether them up in a bag.
I'd sing *chim chiminey, cher-oo!*
I'd sing *oh, the pirate's life for me!*

World, remember how I sneezed in the dust
of the lawn mower shack when that boy climaxed?
Remember how he smiled, as though he'd done
enough? As if. I broke him out in hives and said, *Roberto,*
this splotch looks like Ethiopia and Ethiopia
thrived. Then, basketball documentaries thrived and
the muscle you gave the sun opened wide except

when it was sore.
During those times, you proffered cloud gauze
and I placated with clichés:
Oh sun, I said, *your rays are fingertips upon my*
    windowpane,

like tears and rain and love.
The sun felt better.

Despicable, distinguished World, let me be clear:
I loved Briar more than just as mine. But my love
was an adolescent mongoose in a purse.
My love was three dead, wet mice massing together
in a plastic bag, three fleshy tails entwined.
This is not a metaphor.
Even to you, World, I did not show the parts
where I took off his shoes and cleaned
his feet with window rags. Where I cried because
he flew to Texas for an Astros game.

World, we have so many
worlds inside us. Resurrection daunts.
I would like one last Mexican grill, green
peppers slightly singed. World, you are the
charwoman in Kafka, arms folded over
your breasts, laughing at the bug boy's folly.
I am the apple in the bug boy's splintered back.
Who never knew I was tender. Who never knew
my scent until I withered.

Tanka in a Small Room

Tanka in a small room,
crouching in a corner
eating peanut shells. Briar
on the bed, a fish bowl
in his lap. In the bowl
a fighting fish, looking
for a bar of light to gush
through.

Tanka in a small room,
grass mongreling between
her teeth, a harelip
spreading from her upper
lip down her neck, her
hip, her knee. She splits
into a stuttered beat, into
indelible riffs, and all the
subway tokens in the world
tumble out of her.

Tanka in a small room
crossing Tuesdays off a
calendar. The men on
the balcony in fish paper
shawls aren't helping any.
Briar cuts lengths of vine
to build a raft. Two boys

roll a ball between them,
legs spread, soles pressed
together. Tanka palms
the walls. The men on the
balcony aren't helping any.

Tanka in a small room
making up one gesture
to celebrate all holidays
at once. She jumps like
a bunny, clicks her heels
like Washington, chomps
a Yule log and scuffs some
blood into the floor. Merry
Everyone!

Tanka in a small room. A
stray dog limps in the open
door, kelp between its
teeth. Twisted in the kelp is
more kelp to remind her of
all the sea-less babies who
live in dugout houses. Who
paint snow blindness and
dream in white and white.

(Being in a small room
with Tanka is just a feeling
on the eyeball. A slight fizz

that grows black and blinds
so that the world is dark
but also cool dry tinfoil.
And your eyelids do not
work. Your eyelids are
swept away to a town the
angels make for you. Once
there, you scoop bread
pudding from banana
leaves and grin.)

Tanka in a small room.
Every carnival goes by.
Tanka trolls her hand
out the window to catch
the collar of a clown. She
pulls his face to the bars,
pushes her tongue in his
mouth, and leaves the zip
of battery throbbing in his
gut.

(The eyelid city is reached
by following the screech of
monkeys and the bend of
royal blue in the peacock's
neck. One eyelid is a chair
and another is a cup and
another is a blanket. This is
the softest skin.)

Tanka in a small room
with one hotel placemat,
two open packs of sugar, a
small red plate, and sixteen
spoons. Far away from her,
men moan. The air is so
holy they don't know how
to move it.

Tanka in a small room.
God gone. Briar in the
room next door tying a
cape around his neck. His
fingers shake. The cape was
copped from the seat of a
trike on the boardwalk, left
by a boy who now sticks
bits of cotton candy to his
toes. His mother fiddles
with her halter clasp and
eyes the churro vendor.

(Pull the eyelid over you.
The small room of the
world is now a woman
emerging from her bath
on tiptoe. Her pink veins
do not follow gravity
but bliss to every edge.
A drop of water slides

down the inside of her
calf and settles to rest
below her ankle bone. A
beacon feathers a certain
hill with light. Who lives
beyond the hill? And who
beyond?)

Tanka fills the fish bowl
up with sand and bids
the room good-bye. To
do this she must make
each thing disappear. The
dog. The kelp. The small
boy entering the sea, the
fighting fish, Briar beating
out her smile from his
chest, his raft, the clown,
the men in fish paper
shawls not helping any.
Briar's two broad thumbs.

All of it disappears and nothing miraculous occurs. No
religion follows her. Briar buys a jade plant and covers
its roots with coffee beans. But he is also gone. Everyone
moves. Everyone is white and white. Tanka in a small
room. All the doors are open. All the doors are opening.
The wind from Newfoundland touches the wind of
Istanbul and whines.

Author's Acknowledgments

Thanks to Adam Golaski for being the very first reader of Tanka and for asking to see more. Thanks to Lauren Haldeman, Dina Hardy, Kristin Hatch, Mia and Nico Alvarado, Zach Savich, Luke Sykora, and Lindsay Coleman for offering friendship and wisdom along the way. Thanks to Dean Young and Mark Levine. Thanks to Joanna Klink, brilliant teacher and brilliant poet in equal measure. And finally a huge thank you to Kiki Petrosino, Mary Ann Rivers, Ruthie Knox, and all the folks at Brain Mill Press for giving Tanka a real chapbook to inhabit with all of her venom and mirth.

About the Author

Kaethe Schwehn's first book, *Tailings: A Memoir,* won the 2015 Minnesota Book Award for creative nonfiction. Her poetry and prose have appeared in journals such as *jubilat, Crazyhorse, New Orleans Review, Women's Studies Quarterly,* and *Word for /Word.* Schwehn has been the recipient of a Minnesota Arts Board grant, a Loft Mentor Series Award, and the Donald Justice Poetry Award. She currently teaches creative writing at St. Olaf College in Northfield, Minnesota.

Credits

Author	Kaethe Schwehn
Editors	Kiki Petrosino, Ruthie Knox, and Mary Ann Rivers
Proofreader	Beaumont Hardy Editing
Cover Photography	Leann McDaniel
Cover Design	Stray King Design
Interior Art	Ann O'Connell
Interior Design	Williams Writing, Editing & Design

Brain Mill Press would like to acknowledge the support of the following patrons:

Noelle Adams

Rhyll Biest

Katherine Bodsworth

Lea Franczak

Barry and Barbara Homrighaus

Kelly Lauer

Susan Lee

Sherri Marx

Aisling Murphy

Audra North

Molly O'Keefe

Virginia Parker

Cherri Porter

Erin Rathjen

Robin Drouin Tuch